THE APPLE
LIFE SKILLS
ACTIVITIES

By Terry Perkins

Cover design by Terry Perkins

Printed in the United States of America.
Library of Congress

The Apple

Does not fall far from the tree.

You feed them,

You nurture them,

You watch them grow.

About the Book

The books—The Apple Book, What Is Your Name, and Whose Life Is It Anyway—are user-friendly tools for everyday life skills. They promote positive decision -making for working through personal problems. These books also open a valuable line of communication between youth and adults —about secrets, the importance of eating a good breakfast, bullying, peer pressure, and a wide range of other topics. Author Terry Perkins believes that everyone has a philosophy on life, and his is quite simple: first we are taught, and then we must teach, regardless of our cultural or religious beliefs. Change will come in a child's life, and for anyone to get anywhere in life, teaching must start at home. This book is the first in a three-volume set: volume 1: *The Apple,* is for readers aged six through nine; volume 2: What Is Your Name is for readers aged ten through thirteen; and volume 3: *Whose Life Is It Anyway* is for readers aged fourteen through eighteen. If we don't teach our children at a young age that it's okay to talk to their parents and teachers about their everyday problems, then who will they talk to? Those on The streets and the Internet, or strangers. Instead, I hope your child chooses you!

This book is intended to help those who may not be able to help themselves.

"Some of the topics in this book should be addressed with a parent or adult."

To my mom and dad and family: my brothers and sisters, Ivy Denise, Denarco, Dana, Gina, Derek, Tanya, and Tracy. To my sons, Terry, Marlin, and Terron, and my grandson, Dionta Spells. To Erika L. Beverly and family, Donnell, Ladecha, Erick, Jamiliah, Jamiah, Jamaka, Trina, and Estelle Hays, as well as Angie Burbank and Jacara Burbank. Thanks to all my other friends and family, especially Karen T., Shara T., Joann T., and Gwen L. Peace to all. I'm trying to make a difference one book and one child at a time.

And a very, very special thanks
to Mrs. J. W. Schoyer and Ms. Carmella Pucci
for showing me love from the moment I walked in the door.

Draw a picture of your family.

Did you give anyone a hug today? YES/NO

Did anyone give you a hug today? YES/NO

Date / /

Contents

THIS IS <u>YOUR</u> BOOK.

Please put your name below.

Write your emergency phone number on the second line.

Do this with a parent or an adult.

_____

_____

Date / /

What are you, a boy or a girl?

Draw a picture of yourself.

Date / /

Let's Talk About
WHERE YOU LIVE

What city do you live in?

_____

What state do you live in?

_____

Do you like where you live?

_____

Do you feel safe where you live?

_____

Where would you like to live if you could?

_____

Date / /

Draw a picture of where you live.

Date / /

Let's Talk About
SHARING

Why is it good to share?

_____

Who do you think you can share with?

_____

What can you share with other kids?

_____

Has anyone shared anything with you before?

_____

When you share your things with someone else, how do you think it makes that person feel?

_____

Date / /

Let's Talk About
YOUR NEIGHBORS

Who are your neighbors?

_____

What are your neighbors' names?

_____

Do your mom and dad get along with your neighbors?

_____

What are your neighbors' ethnicities?

_____

Do you have more than one neighbor?

_____

Do your neighbors have any kids?

_____

Do your neighbors have children who you can play with?

_____

Do you fight with your neighbors' children?

_____

Do you feel you can trust your neighbors?

_____

Can you go over to your neighbors' houses after school when there is no one home at your house?

_____

Date / /

Let's Talk About
YOUR BROTHERS
AND SISTERS

How many brothers do you have?

_____

Spell the number out.

_____

How many sisters do you_have?

_____

Spell the number out.

_____

Date / /

Draw a picture of your brother, your sister, or a friend.

Date / /

Let's Talk About
MANNERS

What are manners?

_____

Where can you learn good manners?

_____

What are good manners?

_____

What are bad manners?

_____

When should you use good manners?

_____

Date / /

Let's Talk About
YOUR PET

Do you have a dog?

_____

What is your dog's name?

_____

Do you have a cat?

_____

What is your cat's name?

_____

If your pet is not a dog or a cat, what kind of pet do you have?

_____

Do you feel like your pet is part of your family?

_____

Date / /

Draw a picture of your pet or a friend's pet.

Date / /

Let's Talk About
HEROES

What is a hero to you?

_____

Who is a hero to you?

_____

Where can you find a hero?

_____

Who can be a hero?

_____

Do you want to be a hero?

_____

What are some things a hero does?

_____

Date / /

Draw a picture of you as a hero.

Date / /

Let's Talk About
GETTING LOST

If you are out with your parents and you get separated from them, what should you do?

_____

Think about following these steps to be safe in a store:

1. stay in the store. Do not go outside the store.
2. If you are outside the store, go into the store.
3. look for someone who works in the store to help you.
4. look for a store security guard.
5. ask someone working behind the counter to help you.

How can you tell if someone is working in a store?

_____

Date / /

Let's Talk About
NOT PLAYING WITH
MATCHES OR LIGHTERS

What could happen if you play with matches?

_____

If you play with matches, who could you hurt?

_____

If you see someone with matches, what should you say to him or her?

_____

If you see someone playing with a lighter, what should you do?

_____

If you see a lighter on the ground, what should you do?

_____

Date / /

Let's Talk About
THE HOMELESS

Why do you think people live on the streets?

_____

Do you know what "homeless" means?

_____

Do you think homeless people might be sick?

_____

Do you feel sorry for them?

_____

Do you care about them?

_____

How do they make you feel?

_____

Do some of them scare you?

_____

Do you think you should make fun of them?

_____

Do you think you should help them?

_____

Do you think you should give them food?

_____

Do you think you should give them a place to live?

_____

Do you think you should give them clothes to wear?

_____

How do you think you can help the homeless?

_____

Date / /

Let's Talk About
NEIGHBORHOOD POLICE

Do you ever feel like you need to call the police on anyone?

_____

How do you feel about the police where you live?

_____

Do you trust the police in your neighborhood?

_____

How do you think the people in your community feel about the police?

_____

What does a police officer wear?

_____

Date / /

Draw a picture of a police car:

Date / /

Let's Talk About
PUNISHMENT
Do this exercise with a parent or an adult.

What does "punishment" mean to you?

_____

Do you think punishment is fair?

_____

do you think anyone needs to be punished right now?

_____

At what age do you think punishment should stop for you?

_____

When do you think you should be punished?

_____

Is punishment a good thing or a bad thing?

_____

If you are punished for doing something bad, would you do the same thing again?

_____

Is punishment supposed to hurt, or is it supposed to make you feel good?

_____

How long do you think a punishment should last?

_____

What do you think your punishment should be?

_____

Have you ever been punished for doing nothing wrong?

_____

Date / /

Let's Talk About
WHEN YOU DON'T KNOW
WHAT TO DO

When you don't feel sure about something, what do you do?

_____

Who can you ask when you're not sure about something?

_____

When you feel unsure about something, are you still supposed to do it?

_____

Has anyone ever told you that if you feel unsure about something, you can ask them for help?

_____

Date / /

Let's Talk About
ASKING FOR PERMISSION

Who do you think you should ask for permission?

_____

Why do you think you should ask for permission?

_____

When do you think you should ask for permission?

_____

If you ask for permission before you do something, do you think you will get into trouble?

_____

Date / /

Let's Talk About
RESPECTING OTHERS

What does respect mean to you?

_____

Who should you show respect to?

_____

Why should people respect each other?

_____

Who should you always show respect to, no matter what?

_____

Why do you think I should respect you?

_____

Why do you think you should respect me?

_____

Is talking to someone politely a way to show respect?

_____

Should you respect adults all the time?

_____

Can someone make you respect him or her?

_____

How do you think a person can get respect?

_____

Where can you learn about respect?

_____

Should we earn someone's respect before they trust us?

_____

How do you think you can earn someone's respect?

_____

Date / /

Let's Talk About
A GOOD PERSON

Does a good person do bad things?

_____

Does a good person say bad things?

_____

Do you know what a good person might look like?

_____

Do you know what a good person's name might be?

_____

Do you know where a good person lives?

_____

Do you know how a good person might speak?

_____

Do you think a good person will share what they have with other people?

_____

Do you know where to find a good person?

_____

Do you think a good person would be easy to get along with?

_____

Do you think a good person talks about people behind their back?

_____

Do you think a good person uses foul language?

_____

Do you think a good person gossips about other people?

_____

Date / /

Let's Talk About
TELLING THE TRUTH

Who do you think tells the truth?

_____

Why do you think people don't tell the truth?

_____

Why do you think you should tell the truth?

_____

When do you think you should tell the truth?

_____

If you are not telling the truth, what are you telling someone?

_____

Date / /

Let's Talk About
HAVING FUN

What is fun for you?

_____

Where can you have fun?

_____

What games do you like to play to have fun?

_____

Who do you think you can have fun with?

_____

Is getting in trouble having fun?

_____

How long do you think you can have fun?

_____

Date / /

Let's Talk About
FIVE SENSES

Do you know what your five senses are?

1. SEE with your eyes

2. SMELL with your nose

3. HEAR with your ears

4. TASTE with your mouth

5. TOUCH with your hands

Date / /

Draw a picture of your five senses:

Date / /

Let's Talk About
BREAKFAST

Why do you think it's important to eat breakfast in the morning?

_____

How do you feel after you have eaten a good breakfast?

_____

What does Eating a good healthy breakfast give you?

_____

How do you feel if you do not eat breakfast in the morning?

_____

What did you eat for breakfast this morning?

_____

Date / /

Let's Talk About
RULES

Who do you think should make up the rules?

_____

Who do you think the rules protect?

_____

Why do you think we need rules?

_____

Do you think rules are good or bad?

_____

Do you think you should break the rules?

_____

When do you think you should break the rules?

_____

Date / /

Make a list of your own rules.

RULE 1.

_____

_____

RULE 2.

_____

_____

RULE 3.

_____

_____

RULE 4.

_____

_____

Date / /

Let's Talk About
BIRTHDAYS

Why do you think we have birthdays?

_____

When you grow up, what does your birthday tell you about yourself?

_____

When is your birthday?

_____

In what year were you born?

_____

What day were you born on?

_____

In what month were you born?

_____

How old will you be on your next birthday?

_____

What do you want to do for your next birthday?

_____

What is your favorite kind of cake?

_____

What is your favorite kind of ice cream?

_____

What did you do on your last birthday?

_____

Date / /

Draw a picture of your birthday cake:

Date / /

Let's Talk About
WANDERING AWAY FROM HOME
Do this exercise with a parent or adult.

What should you do before you wander away from your house?

_____

What should you do before you leave your house or yard to go to the store?

_____

What should you do before you leave with your friends?

_____

What should you do before you go to the playground?

_____

Date / /

TELL SOMEBODY!

Let's Talk About
HOMEWORK

Why do you think you need to do homework?

_____

Will doing homework help you do better in school?

_____

Where should you do your homework?

_____

Who can help you with your homework?

_____

When is a good time to do your homework?

_____

Should it be noisy when you do your homework?

_____

Should it be dark when you do your homework?

_____

What should you do with your homework when you are finished with it?

_____

Should your homework be turned in on time?

_____

Should your homework be done neatly?

_____

If you do well on your homework, will it make you feel SMARTER?

_____

If you do well on your homework, will it help you do BETTER on your next test?

_____

Who benefits when you do your homework?

_____

Date / /

Ask someone to give you a spelling test.

_____

_____

_____

_____

Let's Talk About
STAYING OUT OF
TROUBLE
Write what you can do at these places to stay out of trouble.

After-School Programs:

_____

Church Activities:

_____

Boys' Clubs:

_____

Girls' Clubs:

_____

Boy Scouts:

_____

Girl Scouts:

_____

Football Programs:

_____

Baseball Programs:

_____

YMCA:

_____

YWCA:

_____

Youth Centers:

_____

Basketball Programs:

_____

Salvation Army:

_____

Community Center:

_____

The Museum:

_____

The Library:

_____

Parks and Recreation Programs:

_____

Swimming:

_____

Summer Camp:

_____

Computer Camp:

_____

The Zoo:

_____

Fishing:

_____

Date / /

Let's Talk About
PLAYING IN THE STREET

What could happen if you play in the street?

_____

Who could get hurt if you play in the street?

_____

Do you think you can get hit by a car if you play in the street?

_____

Do you play in the street because you don't have a playground near your house?

_____

Do you play in the street because your friends are playing in the street?

_____

Date / /

Let's Talk About
THE STOVE

Why shouldn't you play with the knobs on the stove at your house?

_____

When should you touch the stove?

_____

How can you tell if the stove is on?

_____

If you think you smell gas, what should you do?

_____

Can you see gas in the air if you turn the stove on?

_____

Date / /

Let's Talk About
HELP
Do this exercise with a parent or an adult.

If you are at school and you need help, who can you go to for help? Write down their names.

1. YOUR TEACHER.

_____

2. YOUR PRINCIPAL.

_____

3. A SECURITY GUARD.

_____

4. THE VICE PRINCIPAL.

_____

5. A NURSE.

_____

Date / /

Let's Talk About
KEEPING OUR HANDS
TO OURSELVES

Why should we keep our hands to ourselves?

_____

Why should others keep their hands to themselves?

_____

What could happen if you put your hands on someone else?

_____

Do you want other people to put their hands on you?

_____

When should you keep your hands to yourself?

_____

Date / /

Let's Talk About
HOT WATER

What could happen if you play with hot water?

_____

How does hot water feel on your skin?

_____

Can hot water hurt if it's too hot?

_____

Can hot water burn you?

_____

If you get burned by hot water, will you have to go to the hospital?

_____

Date / /

Let's Talk About
MOMMY OR DADDY
OR A CAREGIVER

Do you take out the garbage without your mom or dad having to ask you?

_____

Do you clean up the house without your mom or dad having to ask you?

_____

Do you clean up your room without your mom or dad asking you?

_____

Have you ever made your mom or dad something special in school because you love them?

_____

Date / /

Let's Talk About
HOW KIDS SHOULD TALK TO ADULTS

Who are some adults that you don't like?

_____

How are you supposed to talk to adults?

_____

Are you supposed to swear at adults?

_____

Are you supposed to talk back to adults?

_____

Are you supposed to make fun of adults?

_____

Date / /

Do you know how to tell time?
Draw a clock showing the time you get out of school.

Date / /

Let's Talk About
YOUR SCHOOL

Why do parents send kids to school?

_____

Why else do your parents send you to school, besides learning?

_____

What day is it?

_____

What year is it?

_____

What month is it?

_____

What grade are you in?

_____

What is the name of your school?

_____

Do you know how many kids are in your homeroom?

_____

What neighborhood is your school located in?

_____

What street is your school located on?

_____

What is your homeroom teacher's name?

_____

Do you know your teacher's contact number?

_____

Do you have more than one teacher in your classroom?

_____

Do you know your principal's name?

_____

Who do you sit next to in art class?

_____

Do you like your school?

_____

Were you bad in school today?

_____

Who was bad in one of your classes today?

_____

What did you learn in school today?

_____

How did you get to school today? Did you go by car, by bus, or did you walk?

_____

Who brought you to school today?

_____

Who picks you up after school?

_____

Who is your best friend at school?

_____

Who made you mad at school today?

_____

Who made you laugh at school today?

_____

What was the best part of your day at school today?

_____

What was the worst part of your day at school today?

_____

Did anyone hit you at school today?

_____

Date / /

Draw a picture of your school.

Date / /

Let's Talk About
PEER PRESSURE

What do you think "peer pressure" is?

_____

Who do you consider to be your peers?

_____

Where do you think peer pressure comes from?

_____

Could your peers be your classmates?

_____

Could your peers be strangers?

_____

Could your peers be older than you?

_____

Could your peers be younger than you?

_____

When someone dares you to do something, is that a form of peer pressure?

_____

When someone tries to get you to do something just to be part of the crowd, is that a form of peer pressure?

_____

If someone tries to get you to do something to be his or her friend, is that a form of peer pressure?

_____

If people try to get you to do something and say you are scared if you don't, is that a form of peer pressure?

_____

If someone says, "I did it, now you try it," is that a form of peer pressure?

_____

Date / /

JUST

SAY

NO

TO PEER PRESSURE
And

SAY YES

to doing
the right thing.

Date / /

Let's Talk About
THINGS YOU LIKE
ABOUT YOUR SCHOOL

1.

_____

_____

2.

_____

_____

3.

_____

_____

4.

_____

_____

Date / /

Let's Talk About
THINGS YOU DON'T LIKE
ABOUT YOUR SCHOOL

1.

_____

_____

2.

_____

_____

3.

_____

_____

4.

_____

_____

Date / /

Let's Talk About
GOOD CLASSMATES

What is a good classmate?

_____

How does a good classmate act?

_____

Does a good classmate talk out of turn in class?

_____

Do good classmates run around playing when they are supposed to be taking a nap?

_____

Do good classmates yell out the answers, or do they wait until the teacher calls on them?

_____

Does a good classmate raise his or her hand and ask for permission before speaking?

_____

Does a good classmate start trouble in the classroom?

_____

Does a good classmate listen to the teacher?

_____

Does a good classmate follow the rules in the classroom?

_____

Does a good classmate help others in the classroom?

_____

Does a good classmate hit other classmates?

_____

Date / /

Let's Talk About
GETTING ALONG WITH
OTHERS

What does "getting along with others" mean?

_____

Why is it good to get along with others?

_____

Who do you think "others" are?

_____

Is fighting a part of "getting along"?

_____

Does "getting along" mean arguing with others?

_____

Is arguing a part of "getting along"?

_____

Date / /

Let's Talk About
BULLYING

What do you think you should do about bullying?

_____

What kind of a person do you think a bully is?

_____

How does a bully act?

_____

How does a bully treat other kids?

_____

Do you think the other kids like the class bully?

_____

Date / /

Let's Talk About
MAKING NEW FRIENDS

Write down four things you can do to make new friends.

1.

_____

_____

2.

_____

_____

3.

_____

_____

4.

_____

_____

Date / /

Draw a picture of you and your new friends:

Date / /

Let's Talk About
HELPING OTHERS
Do this exercise with a parent or an adult.

Why should you help others?

_____

When should you not help others?

_____

Has anyone ever helped you do anything before?

_____

How can you help others?

_____

When are you not supposed to help others?

_____

Date / /

What other ways can you help others?

1.

_____

_____

2.

_____

_____

3.

_____

_____

4.

_____

_____

Date / /

Let's Talk About
TEAMWORK

What is teamwork?

_____

How many people can you have on a team?

_____

Do you think working as a team will help you get a job done faster or slower?

_____

Who in your classroom would you pick to be on your team?

_____

Would you put any girls on your team?

_____

Would you put any boys on your team?

_____

Date / /

Draw a picture of you and your teammates:

Date / /

Let's Talk About
STRANGER DANGER
Do this exercise with a parent or an adult.

What does "stranger" mean?

_____

Could a stranger be a man or a woman, a boy or a girl?

_____

What did your mom and dad tell you about strangers?

_____

Are stranger's good people or bad people?

_____

Why shouldn't you talk to strangers?

_____

Why shouldn't you go anywhere with strangers?

_____

Why shouldn't you take candy from strangers?

_____

What should you do if a stranger tells you that your mom said they should pick you up from school?

_____

What should you do if a stranger tries to grab you?

_____

Who should you run and tell if a stranger tries to talk to you?

_____

What should you do if you see a stranger talking to one of your classmates?

_____

Date / /

Let's Talk About
EMERGENCIES
Do this exercise with a parent or an adult.

What is an emergency?

_____

When should you call 911?

_____

Who can you call in an emergency if you can't get through to 911?

_____

Where can you go in case of an emergency?

_____

What should you do if you have an emergency at home and no adult is at home with you?

_____

Date / /

Draw a picture of an ambulance:

Date / /

Let's Talk About
FIRE SAFETY
Do this exercise with a parent or an adult.

What should you do if you see smoke coming from a room at your house?

_____

Do you think you should try to wake everyone up?

_____

Do you think you should run outside to get help?

_____

Do you think you should run to a neighbor's house?

_____

Do you think you should call 911?

_____

Date / /

Draw a picture of your favorite video game.

Date //

What is your favorite toy?
Draw a picture of it.

Date / /

Draw a picture of your favorite sport.

Date / /

What is your favorite animal at the zoo?
Draw a picture.

Date / /

Let's Talk About
ASKING FIRST

Why should you always ask for permission?

_____

What could happen if you don't ask for permission first?

_____

Why shouldn't you touch things that don't belong to you?

_____

What could happen if you ask the wrong person?

_____

If someone brings a toy to school and you want to play with it, what should you do before you pick it up?

_____

Let's Talk About
WHEN OTHERS TALK
TO YOU

How do you feel when other people won't talk to you?

_____

Do you mind when people scream or yell at you?

_____

Do you want people to talk nicely to you?

_____

Do you like it when people complain to you?

_____

Do you like it when people try to explain things to you?

_____

Date / /

Let's Talk About
ACCIDENTS

What is an accident?

_____

Who can cause an accident, besides you?

_____

How can you prevent accidents from happening?

_____

If you have an accident, whose fault is it?

_____

Where do you think accidents can happen?

_____

Why do accidents happen?

_____

Date / /

Let's Talk About
PRINCE AND PRINCESS
FOR THE DAY
SCHOOL ACTIVITY

Who is a prince?

_____

Who is a princess?

_____

We're going to play prince and princess for a day. Ask your teacher or mom or dad to help you pick out the things you may need.

The boys make crowns and robes and the girls make crowns and gowns.

_____

#1.Ask your teacher what things you can bring from home or ask if you will use things in the classroom to glue onto the crowns and clothes.

_____

#2. Ask your teacher if you can bring your favorite towel from home for your robe or gown.

_____

#3.TAKE A PICTURE OF YOURSELF AND PUT IT IN THE BOOK!

_____

Date / /

Draw a picture of you as a prince or a princess:

Let's Talk About
TROUBLEMAKERS

What is a troublemaker?

_____

Does a troublemaker start trouble?

_____

Does a troublemaker obey the rules at school?

_____

Does a troublemaker only want to do what they want to do?

_____

Are troublemakers in trouble all the time?

_____

Do you like playing with troublemakers?

_____

Do troublemakers get scolded a lot?

_____

Do troublemakers start fights?

_____

Do troublemakers have a lot of friends?

_____

Do you think a troublemaker should go on field trips?

_____

Do troublemakers get suspended from school?

_____

Are you allowed to play with troublemakers?

_____

How do your mom and dad feel about you playing with troublemakers?

_____

Date / /

Let's Talk About
ACTIVITIES FOR AT
SCHOOL OR HOME
Do this exercise with a parent or an adult.

1. STRANGER DANGER:

_____

2. IN CASE OF A FIRE:

_____

3. SHARING:

_____

4. TALKING TO GROWNUPS:

_____

5. HELPING OTHERS:

_____

Date / /

Let's Talk About
LISTENING

Are you a good listener?

_____

Do you listen to your mom and dad?

_____

Do you listen to your teacher at school?

_____

When are you supposed to be listening and not talking?

_____

If someone is trying to talk to you while you are playing, do you think you should stop playing and listen to what that person is saying?

_____

Date / /

Let's Talk About
LEARNING NEW THINGS

How can you learn new things?

_____

Why should you want to learn new things?

_____

Why do you think your parents want you to learn new things?

_____

When you learn new things, does that make you feel smarter?

_____

When you learn new things, does it make you feel good?

_____

When you learn new things, does it make you want to learn more new things?

_____

Is it hard to learn new things?

_____

Do you know how many new things you can learn?

_____

Who can you learn new things from?

_____

Where can you learn new things?

_____

How old do you have to be to learn new things?

_____

Date / /

Let's Talk About
FIGHTING

Why do you think people fight?

_____

Do you like to fight?

_____

Do you think your friends like to fight?

_____

How can you avoid fights?

_____

What do your mom and dad think about you fighting in school?

_____

Do you think you should try to break up fights?

_____

Do you think you should help if your friend is fighting?

_____

Do you let other kids beat up on you?

_____

Are you afraid to fight back?

_____

Has someone told you that you shouldn't fight back?

_____

Did someone tell you that you are too little to be fighting?

_____

Are you afraid to go to school because someone said that he or she was going to beat you up?

_____

Date / /

Let's Talk About
SCHOOL SUPPLIES

What are school supplies?

_____

Do you need any school supplies?

_____

What do you think you might need?

_____

Where can you get school supplies?

_____

Are you afraid to let anyone know that you need school supplies?

_____

Date / /

Write a list of your school supplies.

Date / /

Let's Talk About
HEARING

Do you have trouble hearing in school sometimes?

_____

Do you have to ask the teacher to repeat what he/she said?

_____

Are you sure that you are hearing the right things?

_____

Do you hear better on one side than on the other side?

_____

Has anyone ever given you a hearing test?

_____

Date / /

Let's Talk About
SEEING

Do you ever have trouble seeing the board at school?

_____

Do you have to squint your eyes to see some things?

_____

Has anyone ever told you that you might need glasses?

_____

Where do you sit in your classroom at school?

_____

Can you see the board from the back of the classroom?

_____

Date / /

Let's Talk About
UNDERSTANDING

Do you ever have trouble understanding your teacher at school?

_____

Do you think the teacher is going too fast for you in class?

_____

Do you think the teacher is not spending enough time with you in some of your classes?

_____

Is there something or someone distracting you in class?

_____

Are you paying attention in class?

_____

Date / /

Let's Talk About
READING

Do you ever have trouble reading?

_____

Who do you think you can ask for help with your reading?

_____

If you have trouble with your reading, where can you find help if you're not in school?

_____

How do you think you can learn how to read better?

_____

What can you do to help you read better?

_____

Date / /

Let's Talk About
SPELLING

Do you ever have trouble with your spelling words?

_____

Where can you find help with your spelling?

_____

Who can help you at school with your spelling?

_____

Who can help you with your spelling at home?

_____

Which one of your friends can help you with your spelling?

_____

Date / /

Let's Talk About
MATH

Do you have trouble with your math?

_____

Where you can find help with your math?

_____

Can you get help with your math at home?

_____

Who can help you with your math at home?

_____

What computer games can you play to help you with your math?

_____

Date / /

Let's Talk About
WHAT YOU WANT TO BE
WHEN YOU GROW UP
Do this exercise with a parent or an adult.

Choose three goals:

1.

_____

2.

_____

3.

_____

Which goal do you like the best?

Date / /

Let's Talk About
ASKING FOR HELP
Do this exercise with a parent or an adult.

When do you think you should ask for help?

_____

Where do you think you can ask for help?

_____

Who can you ask for help if you feel you need it?

_____

Why should you ask for help if you think you need it?

_____

Do you think asking for help makes you look weak?

_____

Date / /

Let's Talk About
SAFETY RULES
Do this exercise with a parent or an adult.

Who makes safety rules?

_____

Who is supposed to follow the safety rules?

_____

Who are safety rules supposed to protect?

_____

What do I mean when I say "safety rules"?

_____

When should you use safety rules?

_____

Who needs to use safety rules?

_____

Date / /

Make your own sign about safety:

Date / /

Let's Talk About
THINKING BEFORE YOU ACT

What do I mean when I say "think before you act"?

_____

What could happen if you don't think before you do something?

_____

If you run out into the street before looking both ways, what could happen?

_____

If you were told not to touch the stove because it's hot, and you did it anyway, what would happen to your hand?

_____

Date / /

Let's Talk About
PAYING ATTENTION

Why should you pay attention in class?

_____

What could happen if you don't pay attention?

_____

When should you pay attention?

_____

Does paying attention mean playing around?

_____

Does paying attention mean talking while the teacher is talking?

_____

Date / /

Let's Talk About
DOING THE RIGHT THING

What do you think I mean when I say "doing the right thing"?

_____

Who should always try to do the right thing?

_____

Do you think we should all try to do the right thing?

_____

When do you think you should try to do the right thing?

_____

Where should you try to do the right thing?

_____

Date / /

Let's Talk About
FEELINGS

Do you know what your feelings are?

_____

What do your feelings express about you?

_____

Do you think everyone has feelings?

_____

Can you tell how you're feeling by the way you act?

_____

How can you hurt someone else's feelings?

_____

Date / /

Let's Talk About
FEELING SAD

How would your face look if you were sad right now?

_____

Who do you think you could talk to if you were feeling sad?

_____

Who do you think you could call if you were feeling sad?

_____

Where can you go if you are feeling sad?

_____

Why do you think people feel sad sometimes?

_____

What do you think you can do to make yourself not feel sad anymore?

_____

What do you watch on television when you're feeling sad?

_____

What kind of games do you like to play when you're feeling sad?

_____

What food makes you feel good when you're feeling sad?

_____

what is making you feel sad today?

_____

Are you afraid to say what is making you feel sad today?

_____

Date / /

Let's Talk About
TEASING

How do you think other people feel when you make fun of them?

_____

How do you feel when other people make fun of you?

_____

Why do people make fun of other people?

_____

Do you think it's nice to make fun of others?

_____

Do you think you should make fun of others because other people are doing it?

_____

Date / /

Write a list of kids who tease you.

Date / /

Let's Talk About
HOW YOU FEEL TODAY
Do this exercise with an adult or a teacher.

How do you feel about yourself today?

_____

Do you feel happy today?

_____

Do you feel sad today?

_____

Do you feel fat today?

_____

Do you feel skinny today?

_____

Do you feel ugly today?

_____

Do you feel like being quiet today?

_____

Do you feel rich today?

_____

Do you feel poor today?

_____

Do you feel confused today?

_____

Do you like where you live today?

_____

Why don't you know how you feel today?

_____

Is there something you need to talk about today?

_____

Is there something you're not sure about today?

_____

Is there something you need to get off your chest today?

_____

Do you feel violent today?

_____

Do you need someone to talk to today?

_____

Would you feel better if you wrote down what's bothering you today?

_____

Do you feel ashamed about something today?

_____

Are your feelings hurt today?

_____

Date / /

Let's Talk About
IF SOMEONE TRIES TO FORCE
YOU TO DO SOMETHING THAT
YOU KNOW IS WRONG
Do this exercise with a parent or an adult.

What do you think you are supposed to do when someone asks you to do something you know is wrong?

_____

Are you supposed to go along with doing what you know is wrong and tell someone the first chance you get about what you did?

_____

Are you supposed to run away and tell someone?

_____

Date / /

Let's Talk About
FEELING HAPPY

How do you make a happy face?

_____

How do you feel when you're happy?

_____

How do you act when you're happy?

_____

Do you jump up and down when you're happy?

_____

Where do you like to go when you're happy?

_____

What do you like to do when you're happy?

_____

Who do you like to play with when you're happy?

_____

What games do you like to play when you're happy?

_____

Do you have a smile on your face when you're happy?

_____

Do you like to dance when you're happy?

_____

Do you like to run around when you're happy?

_____

Do you like to sing when you're happy?

_____

Date / /

DRAW SOME HAPPY FACES:

Let's Talk About
GRIEVING
Do this exercise with a parent, adult, or teacher.

Why do you think we have funerals and wakes for our family members and friends?

_____

Do you think a wake is a place where you can say your last goodbyes?

_____

After the wake is over, do you think you will see that person again?

_____

Who do you think should go to a wake?

_____

Date / /

Let's Talk About
FEELING LONELY

How do you feel when you're lonely?

_____

Where do you feel lonely?

_____

Do you feel lonely when you're in a crowd of people?

_____

Do you feel lonely when you're out with your friends?

_____

Do you feel lonely all the time, no matter where you are?

_____

Date / /

Let's Talk About
FEELING SPECIAL

Why do you think you should feel special?

_____

When do you think you should feel special?

_____

Who makes you feel special?

_____

Who tells you that you are special?

_____

What can you do to make yourself feel special?

_____

Do you feel special on your birthday?

_____

Date / /

Let's Talk About
FEELING BORED

Do you feel bored when you are playing with your friends?

_____

Do you feel bored when you're home alone?

_____

When do you feel bored?

_____

What makes you feel bored?

_____

What do you do when you feel bored?

_____

Date / /

Let's Talk About
NOT FEELING LOVED
Do this exercise with a parent or an adult.

Have you ever felt like no one loves you?

_____

When you're not feeling loved, how does it make you feel?

_____

What do you do when you don't feel loved?

_____

How does it make you want to act?

_____

Do you try to find love somewhere else? If so, where?

_____

Date / /

Let's Talk About
FEELING APPRECIATED
Do this exercise with a parent or an adult.

What does "appreciate" mean to you?

_____

Do you feel appreciated sometimes?

_____

When do you feel appreciated?

_____

When do you think someone else should appreciate you?

_____

Do you do things so that others will appreciate you for what you have done?

_____

Date / /

Let's Talk About
HAVING YOUR WAY

How does it feel to have your way?

_____

How do you feel when you don't have your
way?

_____

Are you supposed to have your way all the
time?

_____

Do you cry when you can't have things your
way?

_____

If you can't have your way, do you cross your
arms?

_____

If you can't have your way, do you pout?

_____

If you can't have your way, do you feel like running away?

_____

If you can't have your way, do you go and tell someone?

_____

If you can't have your way, do you stop having fun?

_____

If you can't have your way, do you want to stop playing?

_____

If you can't have your way, do you want to fight?

_____

If you can't have your way, are you mad at the whole world?

_____

Date / /

Let's Talk About
DREAMS

Why do you think we have dreams?

_____

Do you think we can have daydreams?

_____

When you daydream, are you asleep or are you awake?

_____

Do you think your dreams can come true?

_____

When do you think you can start working on your dreams if you want them to come true?

_____

When should you not be daydreaming?

_____

What is a good dream for you?

_____

What is a bad dream for you?

_____

Do you ever wake up from a dream yelling?

_____

Have you ever woken up from a dream crying?

_____

Have you ever woken up from a dream sweating?

_____

Have you ever woken up from a dream shaking?

_____

Have you ever woken up from a dream feeling happy?

_____

Date / /

Draw a picture of your good dreams.

Date / /

Draw a picture of your bad dreams.

Date / /

Let's Talk About
FEELING MAD

How do you feel when someone makes you mad?

_____

When you are feeling mad, do you want to be bothered by anyone?

_____

When someone makes you mad, do you want to cry?

_____

When someone makes you mad, do you want to make him or her cry too?

_____

When someone makes you mad, do you want to hurt him or her back?

_____

When someone makes you mad, do you want to beat that person up?

_____

When someone makes you mad, how long do you stay mad?

_____

When you can't have your way, does that make you mad?

_____

When someone doesn't want to share with you, do you get mad at him or her?

_____

When your mom or dad says you can't go outside to play, does that make you mad?

_____

When you get mad, do you ever want to run away?

_____

Date / /

Draw a picture of your mad face.

Date / /

Let's Talk About
LOVE

How do you feel when your mom or dad says, "I love you?"

_____

Has your mom or dad told you that they loved you lately?

_____

Do your mom and dad smile when they tell you that they love you?

_____

Where do you think love comes from?

_____

If you love someone, how are you supposed to treat that person?

_____

How can you show your pet that you love it?

_____

Do you think you are supposed to love everyone?

_____

Where can you find love outside of your home?

_____

Can you love your pet?

_____

Can you love your friend?

_____

Can you love your mom and your dad?

_____

Can you love your school?

_____

Can you love yourself?

_____

Date / /

Let's Talk About
HATE
Do this exercise with a parent or an adult.

Where do you think hate comes from?

_____

What does "hate" mean to you?

_____

Do you think hate is a good thing?

_____

Do you think hate is a bad thing?

_____

**Have you ever told anyone that you hated them
and felt bad about it?**

_____

How does the word "hate" make you feel?

_____

How does hate make you think?

_____

Do you think good thoughts when you are feeling hateful?

_____

Does hate mean you don't like something or someone?

_____

Does hate mean you do like something?

_____

What kind of face do people make when they say they hate something?

_____

Date / /

Let's Talk About
MISBEHAVING
Do this exercise with a parent or an adult.

Where do you see kids misbehaving?

_____

Where have you ever misbehaved?

_____

Why do you think kids misbehave?

_____

Do you misbehave sometimes?

_____

Were you misbehaving because others were?

_____

What could happen if you misbehave in school?

_____

Do your mom and dad like it when you misbehave?

_____

What should you do if you see someone misbehaving?

_____

What kind of punishment should you get for misbehaving in school?

_____

How do people talk to you when you are misbehaving?

_____

Do you like it when people yell at you for misbehaving?

_____

How do your mom's and dad's faces look when you're misbehaving?

_____

Date / /

Draw a picture of your favorite movie.

Date / /

Let's Talk About
BEING GOOD

Why should you be good?

_____

How do people treat you when you are being good?

_____

How do people's faces look when you are being good?

_____

How do people talk to you when you are being good?

_____

How do people's voices sound when you are being good?

_____

Date / /

Let's Talk About
THINKING POSITIVE

What does "thinking positive" mean?

_____

How does thinking positive make you feel?

_____

Is thinking positive a good thing?

_____

When should you think positively?

_____

Where should you think positive thoughts?

_____

If you don't think positively, what could happen to you?

_____

Date / /

Let's Talk About
LYING

Why do you think people lie?

_____

Have you ever told a lie?

_____

How did telling a lie make you feel?

_____

Do you think people lie because they have something to hide?

_____

Who do other people lie to?

_____

What would happen if you lied to your mom and dad and they found out?

_____

Date / /

Write a list of things that could happen if you are caught telling a lie.

Date / /

Let's Talk About
SECRETS
Do this exercise with a parent or an adult.

What is a secret?

_____

Who can you tell all your secrets to?

_____

What is a good secret?

_____

What is a bad secret?

_____

Has anyone asked you to keep a secret lately?

_____

Have any adults asked you to keep any secrets lately?

_____

Have any of your friends asked you to keep any secret lately?

_____

Has anyone threatened you to keep a secret?

_____

Has anyone told you that if you told about something that happened, no one would believe you?

_____

Has anyone ever taken you to a secret place and told you not to tell?

_____

Date / /

Let's Talk About
STEALING

Why shouldn't you steal?

_____

Why shouldn't you take things that don't belong to you?

_____

What could happen if you are caught stealing?

_____

If I catch you stealing at my house, should I let you back into my house?

_____

Why do you think people steal?

_____

Date / /

Let's Talk About
WHY YOU DON'T LIKE
SOME PEOPLE

Why do you think some people don't like other people?

_____

Does a person have to do something to you for you to dislike him or her?

_____

Do kids you know dislike other kids because of where they live?

_____

Do you think people don't like you because of your friends?

_____

Do you think people should dislike you because of your skin color?

_____

Do you think you should dislike people because your friends don't like them?

_____

Do you think you should dislike a person because they are a boy or a girl?

_____

Do you think you should dislike a person because he is a boy?

_____

Do you think you should dislike someone because he or she is smarter than you?

_____

Do you think you should dislike someone because that person isn't as smart as you?

_____

Can you dislike someone one day and then like him or her the next day?

_____

Date / /

Let's Talk About
WHY YOU LIKE
SOME PEOPLE

Do you think you should like people because of what they have?

_____

Do you like people because you can bully them?

_____

Do you like people because they are as smart as you?

_____

Do you like people because they let you have your way?

_____

Date / /

Let's Talk About
WHAT THINGS SCARE YOU
Do this exercise with a parent or an adult.

What does the word "scared" mean to you?

_____

Have you ever scared anyone before?

_____

What kind of movie scares you the most?

_____

Are you ever scared of the dark?

_____

Are you scared when it rains or when you hear thunder and see lightning?

_____

What animals scare you?

_____

What bugs scare you?

_____

Do you put bugs on people to scare them?

_____

If someone put a bug on you, would you be scared?

_____

What have you done to scare people?

_____

When you go to the movies, do you cover your eyes because you're scared?

_____

Are you sometimes scared, but act like you're not?

_____

Date / /

Draw a picture of a scary monster.

Date / /

Let's Talk About
DAILY HYGIENE
Do this exercise with a parent or an adult.

What does the word "hygiene" mean?

_____

How many times are you supposed to brush your teeth each day?

_____

Are you supposed to take a bath every day?

_____

Are you supposed to wash your hands after you use the bathroom?

_____

Are you supposed to wash your hands before you eat?

_____

Are you supposed to brush your teeth when you wake up in the morning?

_____

Are you supposed to take a bath before you go to bed at night?

_____

How will your body smell if you don't keep it clean?

_____

What else could happen if you don't keep your body clean?

_____

What could happen if you don't take care of your teeth?

_____

Where does bad breath come from?

_____

Date / /

Let's Talk About
SLEEP

Why do you think we need sleep?

_____

Do you feel better after you've slept well?

_____

After playing all day, do you sometimes fall asleep when you sit down?

_____

Do you think your body knows when you need some sleep?

_____

Do you think you can stop your body from falling asleep when you are tired?

_____

Date / /

Let's Talk About
WHY YOU ARE UNIQUE

What does the word "unique" mean to you?

_____

Why do you think you are a unique person?

_____

What things do you feel are unique about you?

_____

Should you feel special?
YES, YOU SHOULD FEEL SPECIAL.
There is only one of you on this whole planet.
There is no other person like you, and there
never will be. You should always do the best
you can do and be all that you can be because
you're not a mistake. You are here for a reason.
You just have to find out what that reason is.

_____

Date / /

Let's Talk About
FEELING PROUD

What does the word "proud" mean to you?

_____

Why should you be proud of the good work you do in school?

_____

When should you feel proud of what you did?

_____

Is it okay to feel proud about your work when you know you have done your best?

_____

Is it okay to be proud of your work when you know that you took your time to make sure you did it right?

_____

Date / /

Let's Talk About
CRYING

Why do you think you cry?

_____

Do you sometimes feel like crying when you are mad?

_____

Are you scared to cry in front of other people?

_____

Do you think people will make fun of you if you cry?

_____

Do you cry when you are alone?

_____

Do you cry because your feelings are hurt?

_____

Date / /

Let's Talk About
FEELING IGNORED

What does the word "ignored" mean to you?

_____

When someone ignores you, do you think that person doesn't like you?

_____

Do you like it when someone ignores you?

_____

If someone tries to ignore you, what do you do?

_____

If someone is ignoring you, what do you think that person is trying to tell you?

_____

Date / /

Let's Talk About
FRUIT

Do you think there are vitamins in fruit?

_____

Why do you think fruit is good for you?

_____

Why should you eat as much fruit as you can?

_____

How many times a day should you try to eat fruit?

_____

What kind of fruit do you like the best?

_____

What are some ways to add fruit to your daily meals?

_____

Can you name some colors of different fruit?

_____

Do you think you can just eat fruit for the rest of your life?

_____

If you don't have any fruit around, where do you think you can find some?

_____

What kind of fruit drinks do you like?

_____

Do you know how to make a fruit salad?

_____

When is the best time to eat fruit?

_____

Where is your favorite place to eat fruit?

_____

Date / /

Draw a bowl of fruit.

Date / /

What are some places where you can find fruit?

1.

_____

2.

_____

3.

_____

Date / /

Let's Talk About
VEGETABLES

Do you think fruits and vegetables are the same?

_____

What kind of vegetables do you like?

_____

What colors can vegetables be?

_____

Do you think vegetables should come in cans?

_____

What vegetables do you think grow in the ground?

_____

Do some vegetables grow above the ground?

_____

Do some vegetables grow on trees?

_____

Do you think some vegetables grow underwater?

_____

Do you think some vegetables grow in the wilderness?

_____

What vegetables can be grown in special greenhouses?

_____

What vegetables have vitamins in them?

_____

What vegetables do you think are good for you?

_____

Date / /

Draw some vegetables.

Date / /

Let's Talk About
THE PRESIDENT
Do this exercise with a parent or an adult.

Do you know what the president's name is?

_____

Do you know where the president lives?

_____

Do you know what the president's home address is?

_____

Do you know what street the president lives on?

_____

Do you know the name of the president's wife?

_____

Date / /

Draw a picture of the president.

Date / /

Let's Talk About
OUR COUNTRY'S FLAG

Do you know what colors are on our flag?

_____

Do you know who designed our flag?

_____

Do you know how many stars are on our flag?

_____

Do you know what those stars represent?

_____

Do you know what the stripes represent?

_____

Date / /

Draw a picture of the flag.

Date / /

Let's Talk About
THE PLANET

Do you know the name of the planet you live on?

_____

How do you feel about our planet?

_____

How can you help keep our planet clean?

_____

What can we all do to help keep our planet clean?

_____

Who can you write to let them know you care about our planet?

_____

Date / /

Draw a picture of the planet.

Date / /

Let's Talk About
SMOKING

How old are you supposed to be before you are able to smoke?

_____

Are you supposed to smoke just because your friends smoke?

_____

Do you like the way cigarettes smell?

_____

Do you know how cigarettes taste?

_____

Do you know how cigarettes affect your lungs?

_____

Date / /

SECONDHAND

SMOKE

KILLS

Date / /

Draw a picture of what you think healthy lungs look like.

Date / /

Draw a picture of what you think unhealthy lungs look like.

Date / /

What instrument would you like to learn to play one day? Draw a picture of that instrument.

Date / /

Let's Talk About
ALCOHOL

What is alcohol?

_____

Who do you think is allowed to drink alcohol?

_____

At what age do you think you are allowed to start drinking alcohol?

_____

Do you think you can get addicted to alcohol?

_____

Do you think alcohol is a drug? YES OR NO

_____

Date / /

Let's Talk About
ILLEGAL DRUGS

Do you think you have a choice to use or not use illegal drugs?

_____

Did you know that some people get addicted to illegal drugs and can't live without them?

_____

Why do you think some people use illegal drugs?

_____

Can illegal drugs turn good people into bad people?

_____

What can happen if you use illegal drugs?

_____

Where do you think you can end up if you use illegal drugs?

_____

How do you think illegal drugs will make you act?

_____

What are some things that you think illegal drugs can make you do?

_____

Do you know some of the ways that illegal drugs can make you think?

_____

What kind of person do you think you will become if you use illegal drugs?

_____

Do you know how you will treat other people if you use illegal drugs?

_____

Date / /

Let's Talk About
GUNS

Why shouldn't kids play with real guns?

_____

Who should leave a real gun lying around?

_____

How can you tell if a gun is real?

_____

What can happen if you play with guns?

_____

Who can get hurt by guns?

_____

What should you do if you find a real gun?

_____

Date / /

GUN'S DON'T KILL; PEOPLE KILL.

THINK ABOUT IT.

STOP THE KILLING.

Date / /

Notes

_____

_____

_____

_____

_____

_____

Notes

Notes

Notes

Notes

About the Author

Terry Perkins believes in family. He's a father, a brother, a grandfather, a friend, and a veteran of the United States Army. He believes that communication is critical in all our lives. If we can't freely express our feelings and our opinions without feeling ashamed as adults, what kind of message are we sending our children? Perkins hopes his books will help foster communication in our homes, our schools, and our streets, and let our children know that violence is not the solution to any problem. Perkins is trying to make a difference one book and one child at a time.

www.ingramcontent.com/pod-product-compliance
Lightning Source LLC
Chambersburg PA
CBHW081348280526

45788CB00009B/2802